The
KEY *of* KINGS

How To Determine Your Own Destiny

By

Guy Finley

Foreword by Ken Roberts

Publishers
Grants Pass, Oregon

ISBN 0-9629127-3-5

The
KEY *of* KINGS

TABLE OF CONTENTS

EXERCISES

An Important Message From Ken Roberts

Great men are they who see that spiritual is stronger than any material force, that thoughts rule the world.

— Ralph Waldo Emerson

*T*his special book is a bridge. It's a bridge from where you are right now to where you'd like to be. Now that you've read and been introduced to the rare and powerful ideas that Vernon Howard presents so clearly and succinctly, you have a choice: You can *act* on these life-changing principles, or you can return to your old way of living. You now stand at the very same intersection Robert Frost found himself at and later wrote of:

*T*wo roads diverged in a wood, and I —
I took the one less traveled by,
And that has made all the difference.

— The Road Not Taken, 1916

To aid in your decision to take this new path and

---

change your life, best-selling author Guy Finley wrote this guidebook exclusively for members of the RICH MAN'S SECRET™ Course. He created it so that you may make the transition from ideas to actual experience. It's specifically for those who want to *cross* the bridge . . . .

These pages contain practical exercises on, and special insights into, the higher principles and ideas you're learning in the RICH MAN'S SECRET Course. In this way, a bridge of understanding is created from where you presently are to the new life you seek. As you apply and incorporate these lessons, the changes you desire begin to manifest.

Countless millions have read the thousands of self-help books written through the ages, yet not much has changed. Very few ever experience the transformation they seek, so what do they do? They read another book, then another . . . and most give up out of frustration.

Answering this common dilemma is the purpose of the RICH MAN'S SECRET Course. Specifically, the weekly INSIGHT LINE commentaries, the monthly INSIGHT LINE Bulletins, and this KEY OF KINGS guidebook work in concert to bring to life for you the higher principles presented in the Course. They are indeed a bridge from mere thought (concepts) to the all-powerful *understanding* you seek.

The analogy is a good one: Learning these new ideas and principles in the RICH MAN'S SECRET Course is like walking through sand — you move more slowly yet expend more energy than usual. Keeping this fact in mind, the following are special encouragements to help keep you on track and reach this new understanding.

The following may sound a bit unusual, or even

foreign, but suspend your questioning momentarily for the sake of this unique opportunity to learn something truly new.

The answer you now seek is not yet within your understanding. If it were in your mind, you wouldn't be seeking! Seeing that this is so is to realize that you are presently limited. But this should not be discouraging — it's the first necessary step in the process of advancing.

Think about tying a shoelace. Now consider writing out a set of instructions for tying shoelaces. Seems overwhelming — almost an impossibility — doesn't it? But five-year-olds rather quickly learn to tie their own shoelaces in spite of the odds. Why? Because they don't think about the intricacies of the job they're undertaking, they just naturally respond to this paramount wish to tie their own shoelaces. *That one wish* is all they need to accomplish their desire.

And your wish to succeed attracts all you need to progress too. Don't expect to immediately succeed at the exercises herein; merely want to! The mere application of any exercise in this book — just your simple act of beginning — sets the discovery process into motion.

At this moment, your mind tells you there's an answer you need to know. But we've already seen that a mind searching for an answer doesn't know what it really needs. So again, suspend that certainty that tells you what it needs to end its uncertainty (!) and focus instead on your original simple wish to learn something fresh and new.

Stay with your desire to understand. Take first things first.

The pilot of an airplane has one job, and one job only, before his vehicle is indeed an aircraft. Before his vehicle can perform to its fullest and do all that it was designed to do, it must first become airborne.

As its tires leave the runway, the vehicle achieves what's called rotation, which means it has just become an aircraft and now exists under an entirely new set of laws and principles. While sitting on the ground, that little airplane can dream and plan and desire all it wants — faraway places, doing loop-to-loops, enjoying the freedom of flight. But the ever-present fact is, it must first rotate and put itself under the influence of the laws of flight that are always and ever-present. *And this all begins with one simple wish . . . .*

—Ken Roberts

The Seed Is The Tree

Thoughts . . . turn to acts
And habits are formed,
From habits the shape
Of character's borne . . .
. . . In character's forged
Each soul's destiny,
So does Truth make plain
The seed . . . is the tree!

— Guy Finley

A Welcoming Encouragement
From The Author

$\mathcal{L}$earning how to determine your destiny is not like learning to repair a clock or master a new language. But we all know it requires time and effort to develop and perfect even such fairly common skills as these.

That's why you must be patient with yourself. And with this brand new study material you're about to read, I assure you that your patience will be rewarded.

In the pages that follow, you will encounter some ideas and insights it's likely you've never considered before. In fact, I'm sure of it. The Keys in this book are to inner doors that few have ever suspected existed . . . let alone had thoughts to open and enter. But you *can* succeed. In fact, you may not know it as yet, but you've already taken your first steps towards something Higher. How? Just by having this material in your hands, your destiny is already new and different. I'll explain.

That part of yourself that led you to acquire this book already belongs to an existing Higher Line of Destiny within you. That's correct. The wish itself to be a Higher man or woman, comes to you from a Higher place and is received in its inner equivalent within you. This means there's *already* an existing connection between the you that you want to be, and what you presently are; between the destiny you would have, and the fortunes you've known. So, all you have to do is stay on that Royal Road that has brought you up to this very point. It leads directly to the Higher destiny you seek. And now, you're about to begin another leg of your appointed journey.

There's so much just ahead of you that's new and exciting. But, you must also remember that the best views are always the higher ones, whose new heights take personal effort to achieve. So, to insure that you'll make steady progress along this Higher Way, allow me to instruct, and encourage, you in two special ways.

First: As you proceed with these new inner life lessons, you may come to certain moments where you have a disquieting feeling that you don't understand what you're doing — or even why you're doing it. But, each time you get ready to throw your hands up in the air, or toss in the towel, remember the following. For here is the true perspective on times such as these: *They are good moments, not bad ones!* In fact, you've been working for *these **very** moments*. And here's why: Your confusion indicates that you've reached the threshold of something *genuinely new to you.* This is the same as a new door to a new destiny. So take heart!

Second: If you'll simply persist with your journey, you'll pass right through these times of trial. I guarantee it. Nothing can stop your sincere inquiry, including those thoughts and feelings telling you that you can't go any farther because you don't understand how to take the next step. Take that step anyway. *Then* you'll understand.

The Light from one small moment of honest self-inquiry is more powerful than the accumulated darkness of a million years of doubt. So, proceed and succeed!

—*Guy Finley*

A Special Invitation To Be One Of The Few

*F*or as long as men and women have walked this Earth, they've been unlocking the mysteries of the world around them. It is our nature to delve, to discover, to push the limits of the known. One by one, from fire to fusion, we have patiently, but persistently, coerced Mother Nature's great secrets out into the open and into our service.

But for all of our insights and conquests over the forces of life around us, we are still living very much in the dark when it comes to understanding the nature of those forces which dwell *within* us.

What about this uncharted world within? What do we really know of its oceans of surging emotions? Of its countless invisible forms of thought? And yet, when put to question, few are troubled to admit it's these same unseen forces at work in this inner world that actually determine the way in which our outer one turns. Which makes the following all the harder to understand: Why does this essential world, which exists in the very heart of us, go unsought and so superficially examined? With so much to gain; with so many powers to be uncovered like layers of treasure in a sunken chest, why are there so few who will dare to probe — and so possess — all of the breath-taking and self-empowering secrets of their own innermost self?

This book is your invitation to be one of the few.

In your hands are all of the instructions you need to make the journey to this invisible world within and, upon your safe arrival, to take possession and command of your own thoughts and feelings. What an adventure awaits you!

In our travels and studies together, we're going to find out why so much of our daily direction seems to come out of default; why it seems that when we really want to do — or be — something truly new and different, we almost always wind up doing just the opposite; where instead of meeting the greater challenge, we find ourselves taking the path of least resistance, and then either blaming someone or something for our condition; or else sadly resenting ourselves for our own weakness.

If you've had enough of being too much for yourself, *The Key Of Kings* holds all the tools you need to discover, and then call upon, a new Source of Strength that will make you the ruler of your own life. In this book you'll be given the secret keys that put you in command of your life journey, as well as all of its experiences. *You will learn how to determine your own destiny.* There are such secrets. They are real. And they can be yours.

In the eleven powerful inner life exercises that are the body and heart of this book, you'll discover how to become conscious of, and completely master, both the strong and subtle forces that actually determine your life choices. And since it is these life choices, your daily decisions, which ultimately decide your direction in life, becoming conscious of the invisible inner influences that determine these decisions will be the same as taking into your hands the reins of your own destiny. **Repeat**: *You can learn how to be that rarest of individuals **who is always going exactly where he or she wants to be going**; one whose entire life experience — each and every step along the chosen way — never fails to be self enriching. **This is the life that's intended to be your destiny!*** Now let's gather the facts that will deliver its realization.

How To Determine Your Own Destiny

*I*t is a Law; not of man's or of woman's, but of Life: Before you can have a different life; before you can be happier, wiser, more at peace, and in quiet command of yourself, **you** must first be different. *Being* is everything.

What is *Being*?

A moment's consideration helps determine that everything around us has some form of Being. Why is this true? Because *all* physical forms — whether animated or not — are expressions of that One Great Life whose vast intelligent and creative energies are the foundation of all we perceive. So we can reason that even a common rock has Being of a sort. Similarly, all manner of Beings — from rocks to roses — to you and I — *all* unique expressions of this One Great Energy — possess a *nature*.

What gives something its *nature*?

The nature of a rock is determined *entirely* by the natural forces acting upon it. This means its Being is without any choice; which further means that both the rock's nature — *and its destiny* — are, in fact, predetermined. One day it will be dust. That's a part of the *nature* of all things physical.

And neither does the rose, dressed so delicately in its fragrant velveteen petals, have a choice as to its nature. An individual rose can't choose not to have thorns or attract bees. Like the rock next to which it grows, the nature of any rose is a *fixed* expression of its Being.

But Human nature — *your* nature — *is not fixed. It can be transformed.* This amazing quality, the inherent potential mutability of our nature, is what sets us above all of God's countless other creations. And this fact about our unique nature also empowers us in a very special way. *As a feature of our **Being** each of us is created with the power to choose the course of our own destiny.* Let's see how this is possible.

Your **Being** is in a constant process of unfolding. *That* it will unfold is not your choice. **Being** is a gift that came with birth. It *is*. And while **Being** is both the creator and cosmic animator of your individual story, *how* your life, unfolds — the *direction* it takes — is something you *can* influence. It's called making choices. And being empowered to have a real voice in your life-choices is what this book is all about. See if the following doesn't make perfect sense:

Before you can change the course of your destiny, you must first gain access to that secret place within yourself where your own future is being created moment by moment by moment. Yes, there is such a location. It's Real. And yes, you can learn to dwell there and direct your destiny.

This truly timeless place, where all of your life-choices are made for you, is what we understand, in concept, as *the*

Present Moment. But this state of True Now is not just an idea. It's a place of extraordinary and measureless power, for the True Present Moment is actually a Cosmic Seed of a sort, from out of which springs *all* that comes later. And this point brings us to one of our key lessons.

Your close consideration of the following insight, coupled with the new knowledge you've already gained from this study, will bring you one step closer to taking command of your own destiny.

The Present Moment is where our ***Being***, which is a timeless unconditioned energy, meets and animates our ***nature***. Now our ***nature***, on the other hand, lives only in time; meaning it's fabricated from all of our past experiences. Said slightly differently, our ***nature*** is a psychological body of memories and knowledge structured by our social, economic, and religious conditioning.

The Present Moment, where our ***being*** and our ***nature*** *meet, is the instant of our destiny.* And up until now, we've had little real choice in how our fates unfold, because it's always been our nature, our accumulated past with all of its fears, compulsions, and doubts that has been running the show. Just a few more facts will help us to further understand some of the inherent problems built into this unconscious inner condition.

Our present nature is a ***thought nature***. *It must think to know itself.* And because the only way it can know itself is through thought, this mental nature is unable to see that many of its own thoughts *are not what it thinks them to be.*

This sort of slip-up in our psyche is nothing really new to us. For instance, we've all known a certain thought that told us we were strong; or really together; only later to find ourselves badly shocked at the depth of our own self deception. Reality came along, as it always does, and made us see that our image of ourselves was just that: only a thought with no real strength at all!

Repetitive experiences such as these should make it clear enough. Our present nature can't really know when it's reached a bad decision; because in that moment — **as** it's deciding *our* destiny — using *its* confused or misguided understanding — our nature, itself, actually *is that bad choice.* Not only can't it see the forest for the trees, sometimes this nature doesn't even know it's lost in the woods!

Things would be bleak indeed if there were no other choice but to live out the remainder of our lives under the conditions imposed by this limited consciousness. Our day-to-day life-situation wouldn't be too dissimilar from that of being a passenger in a coach drawn by six powerful horses with no driver to steer it! Yes, we would, no doubt, be able to get from one place to the next. But for the whole ride, we would be nervous and uncertain not only about *where* we were headed, but if we would arrive there at all! Sound familiar? I know it does! And our agreement serves to take us on to the next step in our journey. Perhaps the most pivotal one.

The time has come to introduce a third character to the horse and carriage metaphor of the paragraph just past. You're about to be introduced to a force in your own consciousness that, when brought to bear in each and every moment of meeting between your *nature* and your *Being*, produces both the missing driver, *and* the reins you need to direct your destiny.

You can think of this third force that can be at your command as a kind of special window into the Present Moment. It's called **Awareness**. And it is the most unique feature of your nature for the following reason: Your awareness of the Present Moment *is* the Present Moment.

You can, and should, pause here for a moment to breathe some life into this last, very important, idea. To take it out of the realm of thought, and into your direct experience, just choose to come fully aware of yourself. If you've never tried this before, here's some helpful guidance.

Come wide awake to your total environment *this moment*. Just **know**, without *thinking*, what are all of the sounds, sights, feelings, thoughts, impressions, textures and temperatures that may be all around, and within you, *right now*. Again, this knowing yourself, and your surroundings, **is not** arrived at by going into thought. And, if you'll practice this higher kind of self-presence, you'll see that this special awareness of yourself *is the same as the Present Moment* in which you just became aware. They are one and the same. Which means this self awareness, as it includes the Present Moment, is also a feature of your **Being**. This is the inner realization we've been working toward all along.

Your awareness of the Present Moment, which is a secret part of your True **Being**, doesn't have to think about which direction is best for you. *It knows* because *it sees*. Where your usual **nature** is often blinded by its own unseen self interests, your **Being**, represented in the moment by your awareness of it, effortlessly sees into — and through — this unconsciously compromised thinking even as it's occurring.

The presence of this Higher Intelligence keeps you from defeating yourself. And this is the same as making you newly victorious! For each time you have the awareness **not to choose** from that bank of old patterns produced by your limited thought nature, new and higher alternatives appear before your inner eyes. These moments and their messages rise to greet you from your True Being. And with these directions as your guide, your Higher Destiny is assured. After all, they are coming to you from Reality Itself.

Taking The High Road
That Leads To Self Rule

*F*ollowing this last, brief chapter section, you will be introduced to eleven exercises designed to help you determine your destiny. Each one has unique properties and presents a special challenge that will help you awaken new levels of higher self awareness. With alert practice you'll soon possess the power to change the direction of your life — by changing your *nature* — as it expresses itself in the Present Moment.

For best results, read the following eleven individual exercises all the way through, just as you would read through any book from start to finish. Then, return to the individual lessons by making each one of the exercises the focus of your undivided study for at least a full day. For superior results, I suggest you work with each exercise for one complete week. Take longer if you like. But, regardless of your elected length of practice time, make every effort with each exercise to work with its particular inner lessons at every available opportunity . . . of which you're sure to find dozens in any 12-hour period.

Start with any one of the exercises you would like.

Maybe there will be one that better suits your personal situation at the moment than any of the others. That's fine. But whichever of the exercises you choose to begin your inner work, it's important that you work your way all the way through each of the eleven. And here's one last suggested instruction that will help your inner work progress noticeably faster.

As you finish working with one exercise, and prepare to move on to the next, continue with the practice of the one you've just completed. Even though the new exercise on your list will demand most of your attention, you can remain aware of — and continue to work on — these combined studies. You'll discover that the collective effect of these inner exercises supports and amplifies one another in ways that help hasten higher self discovery.

*O*ne last note: Succeed just once — with any of these unique inner life exercises — and *your life will never be the same again.* **All** will be new for you; both for the fact of your victory over your own time nature, and for your new knowing that now tells you . . . **You can change your destiny.**

*S*pecial Summary: There is no such thing as a wasted step when your final destination is self transformation.

Eleven Keys To Help You Change
The Course Of Your Destiny

THE EXERCISES

Exercise # 1
GET ONE THING DONE

Special Insight

Nevermind how much there may be to do; or how hard some task appears to be. *Get one thing done* and then, take that step again. Consciously brush aside any other concerns. Do what's in your power. *Refuse to deal with what's not.*

Exercise and Instruction

Have you ever had this experience? You're faced with so many things that have to be done in a timely manner that it overwhelms you . . . so *all you do is nothing!* Well, that is, *almost* nothing.

You do manage to:

1. Worry yourself sick about how you'll get everything done.

2. Eat or snack until you feel drowsy.

3. Take several naps hoping to awaken inspired.

4. Re-organize your papers and desk drawers as part of your plan of attack.

5. Worry about all of the time you know you've wasted making plans and re-organizing your desk.

If you're tired of finding yourself exhausted — even before you're able to start working on some line of tasks assembled before you — this exercise is custom-made for you. The following insights and prescribed actions will lend just the help you need to succeed in handling a hundred pressing jobs; all while enjoying that inner calm and confidence that comes with knowing — not only are you doing all that can be done — but you're doing it in the best possible manner!

Most of us are familiar with that time-tested, golden adage, "All is not as it appears to be." One of the hard ways we've all learned that this old saying is true is when it comes to certain smiling faces. There's no doubt about it: Appearances can, and often do, deceive.

But we've yet to discover this same wise advice also holds true as it applies *to the appearance of our own thoughts.* Thoughts deceive us all the time. It's true. In fact, we'd never have been deceived by anyone in our lives if we hadn't first been mislead *by our own ideas* about that person. But, it's not just in the area of relationships that our own thoughts deceive, and so betray, us. Which brings us to the key insight underlying this exercise.

At any given moment, regardless of appearance or any emotional certainty to the contrary, it is not the demand of those already-overdue, hundred and one tasks that have you feeling so overwhelmed and under prepared. *What you're really experiencing is the overwhelming presence of **one thought:** One thought that calls itself one hundred and one* *things to do.* Impossible you say? Please, read on.

The power this one thought has to deceive, and to ultimately freeze you in your tracks, is born partly out of its invisible alliance with anxiety-laden emotions. Here's how these two terrible tricksters team up to keep you off track and forever running for the train.

Thoughts have the power to present themselves to your mind in picture form. These thoughts are known to us and experienced as imagination. In this instance, as it concerns our study, one thought assumes the image, or mental picture, of one hundred and one tasks yet to be completed. To illustrate to you how this kind of mental picture is possible, imagine a photograph of a terribly cluttered desk. This mental picture is, in fact, *one* image with a thousand loose ends!

What happens next is that this same, single mental picture, consisting of multiple superimposed images, becomes animated with the aforementioned anxious and pressure-filled feelings. Now, in your mind's eye, that picture of your impossible situation not only looks real . . . it *feels* that way too! But this show has just begun.

In the wink of an eye, a second thought pops up. And unbeknownst to you, it's in league with the initial imaginary scene projected by the first thought. Its task is to confirm your worst suspicions; which it does when it announces in a small, but defeated voice that sounds a lot like your own: "It's hopeless. There's just too much to do. How can I get out of this?"

The next time you "hear" this inner voice of imminent doom, listen instead to this Higher Instruction:

Never again look for a way out of any anxious condition. **Look instead for a way to see through it.**

Now learn the Higher techniques that will show you how to be a self-starting individual instead of a self-stalling one.

Each time you're faced with a log-jam of tasks that seem far beyond your mortal abilities to resolve in the allotted time, here's what to do. First, whittle these logs down to manageable size by writing each one out on a pad of paper. This act will also help you untangle some of your own tangled feelings about the jam you're in. Just forget their order of importance for now. That will become clear later. Just get each pending task down on paper. Besides, your priorities can only be as clear as your thinking, so making this list helps to clarify both. Another benefit of your list is that it will keep confusion out of the picture, and confusion is to anxiety what wind is to a dust-devil.

Once you have your list of tasks written down on paper, place a star next to number one on your list. Then *Do It!* What does this mean? Exactly what it says!

Take number one on your list and just *get that one thing done.* Consciously refuse to entertain any other thoughts that push themselves into your mind with images of impossibility. It *is* possible to *do one thing at a time.* And it *is* possible to successfully *complete* one thing at a time, and to do that one thing to the very best of your ability. Then . . . move onto the next task at hand: Number two. Follow the same winning procedure as you did with number one! Then do number three, and so on, and so on, until all is done.

The main lesson here is that it only becomes

impossible to succeed when you try to deal with *what isn't in your power.* There are renegade parts of you that want you to waste your powers dealing with them. Your misguided attention to their punishing presence gives them a life they wouldn't have without tricking you into giving them one. This means you don't need power to deal with what's been defeating you, only the Higher Understanding it takes to consciously dismiss it from your inner life. You have that power ***Now.*** Start using it.

Work with this exercise. Use its instructions. Get one thing done, one thing at a time, all the way down your list . . . whatever it may be. Proceed in spite of any thoughts or feelings that would have you believe you can't. Just behind your certainty that your "list" is too much for you, lies a new and conscious capability to proceed one step at a time; to accomplish one task at a time; to your satisfaction.

"Doubt is the vestibule which all must pass before they can enter the temple of Wisdom. When we are in doubt and puzzle out the truth by our own exertions, we have gained something that will stay by us and serve us again. But, if to avoid the trouble of the search we avail ourselves of the superior information of a friend, such knowledge will not remain with us; we have not bought, but borrowed it."

— Caleb Colton

Special Summary

The most beautiful tapestry in the world begins and ends with but *one* of a hundred thousand threads.

Exercise # 2
TAKE THE CONSCIOUS RISK

Special Insight

Nothing you're afraid of losing can ever be the source of your fearlessness.

Exercise and Instruction

Question: Has there ever been a time in your life — a period of real self enriching growth — that wasn't connected to a risk you either willingly undertook or — to a time of inner trial where there was no other choice for you but to take a risk? Of course there's only one answer to this question; and it's one recognized as being true wherever you may ask it in the world: The prize of greater wisdom and inner strength always goes to those who take, in one way or another, *the risk.*

But one note before we go any farther. The author is not recommending risking your resources on ridiculous, "get rich quick" financial schemes. Nor is risking your life by trying to cheat death with some harebrained stunt what it means to take a risk. These kinds of activities aren't really risks at all, other than on a very superficial level. Yes, risks like these may give you a temporary charge, but so does sticking your finger in an electrical socket! Real self change goes far beyond merely boosting self esteem. It's a permanent inner transformation that frees you from ever feeling low in the first place.

This exercise is specialized instruction, a Higher Education, in how it's possible for you to find — and then willingly enter into — **Conscious Risks.** With what you're about to learn, you won't have to wait for an accidental, or painful, event to come along and prompt you into realizing a self liberating self change. You'll be empowered with a secret knowledge that will actually allow *you* to choose these moments of self transformation. You will have a hand in creating your own destiny and ultimate spiritual success.

· Let's take the needed moment to briefly review exactly what is a conscious risk? And also, why these kind of risks can be such a powerful catalyst for inner change. Then we'll learn how to locate these special risks at will, including the winning actions to take when these moments of conscious risk present themselves. But first, a definition:

A conscious risk involves making a choice to do what's true, in spite of what that choice may cost you.

One fairly common example of this uncommon kind of inner valor is refusing to go along with the destructive behavior of someone you love . . . even though that choice may mean he or she walks out of your life. But, even here, the victory is still yours. For even in worst-case scenarios, you always discover that *what you lose is **never** the thing you feared losing.*

Yes, that self destructive man or woman may be gone

for good, which hurts at first. But it's not too long before *you know* something *else* is missing too. What you really lost was a part of yourself that had been a secret slave to a false image of what it means to be loving — or to the fear of finding yourself alone. And as this revelation strengthens, which it always does, you finally can see that all you really lost was a source of unconscious sorrow you'd always mistaken for being *you*! What a relief.

These discoveries deliver into your hands a personalized invitation to find what is your own free and fearless life. We can summarize our study to this point as follows: On the other side of any conscious risk is the *realization that **who you really are** has nothing to fear.* But, in order to make this self liberating discovery, you must willingly face those fears, whatever they may be. Here's some extra encouragement.

The moment of real conscious risk always feels like a tunnel with no light at its other end. But, each time *you'll choose to enter it anyway,* that tunnel turns into a bridge spanning the space between your past fearful life . . . and your new fearless one.

In the forthcoming list are various examples of everyday events, each of which presents a unique opportunity to take a conscious risk. And, as you'll see, even the most common occurrences hide within themselves secret bridges to new self wisdom and greater inner strength.

1. Risk Saying No

The first step towards having your own free life begins with daring to refuse the silent demands of others. Saying "yes", for fear of saying "no" is a recipe for resentment. Risk walking away from fear. Say "no".

2. Risk Leaving Empty Spaces Empty

Giving yourself empty things to do can't fill that emptiness you feel inside. So risk leaving that space empty. Allow it to fill itself, which it wants to do, with something you can't give yourself: The end of feeling empty.

3. Risk Not Defending Yourself

It's only when you consciously risk laying down your armor, shield and sword; your quips, retorts and criticisms; that you discover who *you really are **can not be hurt***. Risk letting others win.

4. Risk Appearing Stupid

Pretending to understand something you don't, for fear of appearing stupid, only insures that you'll remain a fearful pretender for the rest of your life. And *that* is stupid. Risk asking all the questions you need to ask. *That's* smart!

5. Risk Bearing Your Own Burdens

The weight of any trouble is determined by how much you fear it. But the *only* weight any fear can have is what *you* give to it when you try to push it away. Risk not "sharing" your burdens. Stop pushing them onto others. You'll be amazed how light they really are.

6. Risk Being Rejected

"No" is just a word, but the fear of it is a prophecy self fulfilled. Be bold! Risk asking for what you really want. Reject the fear of being rejected by daring to say "no" to the fear of no.

7. Risk Catching Yourself In the Act

Your life can't be both a show and be real. Catch yourself in the middle of some self created drama and just drop it. Risk bringing the curtain down on yourself. Life is real *only* when *you* are.

8. Risk Taking The Lead

You can never know the true pleasure and spiritual satisfaction of having your own life until you take the risk of finding it for yourself, *all by yourself.* Followers fear to tread that Higher inner road called "My Own Way". Risk going out in front.

9. Risk Letting Go

You've been trying to run your own show, and so far, it's pretty much been just a nightmare with entertaining intermissions! Risk letting something Higher have Its Hand at directing your life. Let your show go.

10. Risk Being No One

Everyone wants to be seen by others as being great. This makes that kind of greatness common. Be awake to what is common in your life and then risk doing the opposite. Real Greatness follows.

Best of all, look for your own moments where taking a conscious risk will lead you to a liberating self discovery. Here's a helpful hint to get you started looking in the right inner direction.

In olden days, prospectors searched for gold which was then plentiful along river banks and in the exposed beds of mountain streams. Besides knowing how to look for the right geological formations, where it was likely gold nuggets lay hidden just under the sandy gravel, the best prospectors also had a special trick up their sleeve that helped shift the odds of finding gold in their favor.

As they walked along the water's edge, they'd place themselves with the sun to their back and watch for a slight glint or golden flash in the sand. They knew from experience that where there were flakes of gold, nearby were the chunks. By following a similar approach in your search for inner gold, you can succeed in this exercise of taking conscious risks. Here's the parallel.

Watch yourself, all the time, wherever you are and whatever you may be doing, for that telltale flash of resistance, anger, frustration, anxiety or fear. Then let your heightened inner awareness lead you to the prize of self liberation.

Since your usual reaction to any negative emotion is *to avoid* the condition or person you think is responsible for that feared feeling, ***your new and higher action is to consciously go towards that flash.*** In other words, don't walk away from what you see as being the source of your negative state; instead, willingly walk toward it. Trembling if you have to! But Risk It!

The priceless inner gold of a fearless life is waiting there just for you.

"What did you do today to receive your instruction?"

— *Louis Pasteur*

Special Summary

True strength is the flower of Wisdom, but its seed is action.

Exercise # 3
CANCEL SELF WRECKING RESENTMENTS

Special Insight

Whatever form they may take, your resentments wreck only you . . . **not** the one you resent.

Exercise and Instruction

Two men stroll down a leaf-covered woodlot path on a clear, brisk Autumn morning. Jeff and Mark have been friends for years. They enjoy their Saturday morning walks and talks together. Yet, something's different about Mark today. Jeff senses there's a problem. But he says nothing.

Two minutes later Mark stops walking, and turns to Jeff. His eyes are searching for a place to begin. Then, following right behind his slowly spreading smile, these words spill out: "Jeff, are all these voices that are arguing in my head bothering you too?"

A second later, they both break out laughing. The spell Mark had been under was broken. He had been the captive of a *dark inner dialogue.*

What's a dark inner dialogue? Just what it sounds

like: a negative tug-of-war in the unseen recesses of your mind where you're the only one pulling on both ends of the rope. Still more to the point: Being in a dark inner dialogue *is finding yourself losing a heated argument when there's no one else in the room with you!*

What causes these dark inner dialogues? Resentment. So, here's a key thought to help you release this self wrecking inner state: Holding on to some hurt, or hatred — over what someone may have done to you in the *past* — makes *you* that person's slave *in the here and Now.*

If you're tired of being a slave to a painful relationship out of your past, this study and exercise in how to release resentments is sure to bring welcome relief.

For this lesson to succeed in its intended purpose, it's important for you to understand that resentment is a bitter pill made up of *two* layers. The first layer is created by our refusal to be self ruling: Saying "yes", when we really want to say "no!" is one good example. Fawning before others for fear of their reprisal is another. Both weak actions breed resentment, because our wish to falsely accommodate compromises our natural need to be self commanding.*

The second layer of this type of resentment is its "active" ingredient; the psychological component that keeps it alive and not well. This is the *dark inner dialogue.* These unconscious conflicts, in dialogue form, play themselves out in our mind by painfully reenacting

* Secret Way Of Wonder, Guy Finley. Llewellyn, 1992

various scenes from our past; moments gone by in which we either know, or sense, we were compromised by our own weakness. And now comes another key thought.

If these inner dialogues were left to themselves as they popped into our mind, they'd be as powerless to disturb us as an echo is to change its own sound. Where we get into trouble, when resentment rules, is when we're unknowingly drawn into these scenes out of our past and find ourselves interacting with a cast of ghost players! The ensuing mental dialogue is always a desperate, but futile, attempt to change *what has already* been said and done — so that maybe this time around — we can come out a winner. One good example of this kind of dark inner dialogue is giving someone a heated piece of your mind, *when he or she is not around to hear it!* Tired of going twelve rounds in routine fight scenes that always turn out the same? Try this new exercise for the winning solution.

If you sat down on a metal bench and suddenly realized the mid-day sun had heated it way beyond the comfort zone, you'd stand up as quickly as you could. The same Intelligence behind this instinctive physical reaction can help you release all resentments and drop their dark inner dialogues.

Each time you can catch yourself in a dark inner dialogue **of any kind**, use your awareness of the conflict it's creating within you as a springboard to help you leap out of those scary scenes from your past into the safety of the Present Moment. Then, instead of giving yourself back over to those inner voices of conflict that are still trying to converse with you, just remain quietly aware of yourself in the Present Moment, and of their continuing beckoning presence.

No matter how many times you hear in your mind those fighting words that have always prompted you to jump into that dark dialogue, **refuse to join in.** *Ground yourself in your awareness of the Present Moment.*

The unconscious resentment responsible for creating those heated scenes from the past can not follow you into the **Now,** which means no dark inner dialogue can tag along either. Why? Because when you're no longer a captive of your own past, then you can recognize its ghost voices *as the source of psychic intrusion they really are.*

Remember, no dark inner dialogue can ever solve an unresolved resentment any more than one end of a snake is less the serpent.

"Vengeance is Mine, saith the Lord."

— Old Testament

Special Summary

Learn to ask for a happy, new life, by refusing to re-live what's been tearing at you.

Exercise # 4
STEP OUT OF THE RUSH

Special Insight

Even at a million miles an hour, anxious thoughts and feelings *still take you no-where.*

Exercise and Instruction

Before you can step out of the rush and into your own life, you must first see that while anxious, hurried feelings often lend a temporary sense of self importance, these same racing emotions actually rob you of the power you need to be self commanding. A brief investigation will confirm this finding.

Self command *begins* with being able to choose your own direction in life. And whether you're caught in the raging current of a white-water river, or being swept along by a flood of invisible thoughts and feelings, one fact remains: Like it or not, *you're* going where that current goes. You have no real choices as long as you're under its influence. That's why learning to step out of the rush is the same as learning how to step into your own life.

Allow the following exercise to show you that your

Real Nature never feels the need to rush any more than an eagle would try to swim across a lake to get to the other side.

Here's the challenge: Rushing thoughts and anxious feelings are invisible to you because each time they begin to race, *you start to run with them.* And after so many years of being carried along in this psychic slip-stream, you've come to believe that either **you** are these surging inner currents, or that their power is yours. Neither case is true. You are not these waves of thought any more than a cresting tide is the entire ocean.

Author Vernon Howard offers us this emphatic instruction to help strengthen our resolve to stop this mad dash to nowhere:

"Slow down. Relax. Dare to deliberately defy those inner screams that demand you rush nervously around. Instead, obey another quiet voice that assures you that the casual life is the truly powerful and efficient life."

Now here's the solution in exercise form that will help you to slow down your life.

Beginning this very moment, intentionally separate yourself from any rushing inner condition by voluntarily stepping out of it. How can this be done? ***Purposefully slow yourself down*** by acting to consciously reduce your usual speed. Here are several suggested ways to guarantee a good start.

1. Walk over to get your cup of coffee at 50% your normal gait.

2. Try reaching for the phone, your glass of water or

your pen, at 75% your normal speed.

3. How about driving the speed limit when you're late for an appointment!

One practice I find particularly profitable, at home and in business practices, is to always pause a few seconds before I answer someone's question. "Fools rush in," the saying goes! Whatever the occasion, you choose the time and place to slow down, and then practice stepping out of the rush.

Here's the secret behind how this unique exercise delivers new self command: Slowing down helps you become aware of yourself in a new and higher way by creating contrast between your usual speed through life, and your now selectively slower one. This enhanced self awareness empowers you to step out of the rush by *making you conscious of its flooding presence **within** you as being something that doesn't belong to you.* Once this is clear, then you can choose **your** *own* direction in life. Step out of the rush by slowing down. Do it Now.

"Whoever is in a hurry shows that the thing he is about is too big for him."

— Philip Chesterfield

Special Summary

If you want to find what is Timeless, dare to live as though you have all the time in the world.

Exercise # 5
REFUSE TO BE SELF COMPROMISING

$\mathcal{S}$pecial Insight

Refuse to compromise yourself in the present moment for the promise of a happier one to come.

$\mathcal{E}$xercise and Instruction

Your True Nature is **Now**. There is no later. This means that *before* we can change the unhappy endings in our life, we must learn how to drop them *before* they begin. And yes, this can be done. There is no other possible order; no other real correction for getting to the root of what's been wrecking our days.

This special exercise has the power to change everything about your life for the better, precisely because it's all about changing how the troubling things in your life *really* begin. Your close study of these inner life lessons will reveal to you a hidden story. Then watch how your new vision brings you new victory.

The next time a want of any kind presses into your heart or mind, ask yourself these two questions in the order about to be presented. For best results, take a piece of paper and draw a line down the middle from top to bottom. At the top of the left hand column, write out the following question:

How do I feel about what I want?

Now, at the top of the right hand column, write this question to yourself:

How does this want make me feel?

The first step to take with this exercise is to notice the important difference between these two questions now written at the top of your paper.

Then, in the left hand column, under the question "How do I feel about what I want?", write down any of the thoughts and emotions that go through you as you imagine how you're going to feel when you get the object of this new want. What is it? Perhaps a new job or higher position; a better relationship; or maybe that skirt, shirt, vacation, or car you've been dreaming about driving across country.

What are some of these feelings that accompany such long-awaited wants? I'm sure you can list your own but how about: A) Excitement, B) A sense of well-being, C) The enjoyment of seeing yourself in your mind's eye as the envy of all your friends.

Now, having taken inventory of *how you think you're going to feel* in that near or distant moment, take yourself out of this world of pleasing promises and address the question in the right hand column that asks you to see *how is this want making you feel in the present moment?*

Don't be at all concerned with what you may now discover within yourself. Just quietly observe *all* of those thoughts and feelings secretly attending to your want. Then fill in the right hand column with your insights. What will you write down?

Some of the surprising answers to "How does this want make me feel?" could include feelings such as these: A) Gripping anxiety, B) Disturbing or distant doubts, C) Worrisome fears. What's happening here?

Follow closely: The same mind that projects a pleasure-to-come is instantly, but *unconsciously*, pained that it may not be able to possess that pleasure which it has imagined for itself. This invisible anguish is the root of self compromise; for now we struggle to free ourselves from this self created sorrow by doing "whatever it takes" to realize our wants.

If you will work at this exercise as outlined for you, and consciously apply its principles *each time* one of those familiar, haunting wants arises, you'll understand what few men and women on this Earth have ever known. And this is it: Each present moment is the seed of the next; and it is the actual content of what is occurring *Now* that brings us all that we experience as our life.

Your awakening awareness *to what your wants are actually giving you* will help you to change **what you've been asking from life.** And as your life-requests change in each present moment — from being secretly punishing to increasingly perceptive ones — you'll naturally begin to free yourself from all unconscious self compromising acts.

"He who promises runs in debt."

— The Talmud

Special Summary

You can't be divided *and* be content, so choose in favor of self wholeness.

Exercise # 6
TAKE THE STEP
THAT YOU'RE SURE YOU CAN'T

Special Insight

Each time you'll take the step that you're sure you can't, you'll discover that the "you" who would not *was only a **thought*** that believed it could not.

Exercise and Instruction

How many times have you found yourself thinking you'd like to develop a new skill, or sharpen an old one? Maybe learn a language or musical instrument; further your higher education; or maybe just get up out of your easy chair and do some catch-up on that correspondence you've been putting off for weeks!

But in each, or at least most of these instances, before you can even get started, you find yourself turned back; repelled from your upcoming chosen task by an onslaught of invisible forces! Suddenly you're surrounded by deep weariness, self doubt, mental fog, or sometimes just plain fear. Do you recognize any of these self-stalling inner-attackers? Would you like to be liberated from their limiting influences? Freed to pursue higher levels of your own inner development? That's what this exercise is all about: To teach you how to take that next step each time you're just sure you can't. Let's begin by covering a few basics in Higher, or esoteric, psychology.

Most of us wouldn't be too surprised to hear that our mind has a will of its own. We all know what it's like to be more or less helplessly doing something we wish we weren't! We often feel the presence of this force within, but don't much understand it — or its implications.

Figuratively speaking, every cell of your whole body has a "will" of a sort. This is a well-known scientific truth. Both the mind and the body are always hard at work, at a cellular level, to keep their lives — as they know them — in what is called "homeostasis". Don't let this fifty-dollar word throw you. All it means is, "the tendency of any organism, simple or complex, to want to maintain within itself relatively stable conditions". Translation as it concerns this exercise: There are more parts of you *that want to stay the same* than there are ones interested in growing, or achieving new heights through effort.

The good news is that *who you really are* is greater than any one of these invisible aspects of yourself which are mechanically compelled to maintain its status quo. Your True Nature is greater than the sum of all these physical, mental, and emotional parts. If you have any doubts about this, it's in your power to make this Truth self evident.

The next time you want to go ahead with any project, whether it's designing a rocket ship, or finally getting around to repairing your favorite rocking chair, and you start to feel those old familiar doubts, dreads, or doldrums rising up to block your way, *just walk right through them.* You can do it if you use your new Wisdom to clear the way for you.

For instance, one excellent way to break through these seemingly impassable inner states is to see them as being the fakes which they are. This isn't to say you won't feel their punishing presence when you first dare to defy their threats. But, each time you'll psychologically walk up to — and past — these inner disturbances, you'll become increasingly aware that these task-resistant thoughts and feelings are just big fakes! Of course, you must prove this to yourself to know the powers that come with such a discovery, but here's a glimpse of what you'll learn each time you take that step you're sure you can't.

Those negative states that try to stop you from taking the next step of any chosen journey are just psychological *special effects.* These obstacles of psychic flash-and-smoke are generated by the mind to keep you from disturbing *its* established levels of comfort. But, special effects, regardless of the kind of "screen" upon which they're projected, have no reality outside of your temporary belief in their appearance.

The truth is these inner-barriers are without real substance, and so **must** vanish the moment you pass through them. Which brings us to a great Spiritual Truth: *On the other side of the resistance is the flow.* This means that each time you'll call on this exercise to walk through some pocket of inner resistance, on its other side, you'll find all the fresh energy and intelligence you'll need to go through and complete your appointed task.

All these years you've been taught to believe that before you can hope to succeed at something, you have to first *feel* as though you can. No! To succeed, you need only understand how failure is created, and then consciously refuse to cooperate with what has been defeating you **from within.**

"Every noble work is at first impossible."

— *Thomas Carlyle*

Special Summary

Each step **into** what you think you can't do is one step **further away** from that nature which wants you to think that circles actually go somewhere.

Exercise # 7
BREAK OUT OF THE BLAME GAME

Special Insight

Blaming conflict-filled feelings on any condition, or person, outside of yourself is like getting angry at your shoes for being laced too tight.

Exercise and Instruction

Most men and women recognize the need for a healthy, balanced diet, because good eating habits nourish the body. Good nutrition helps keep us agile and strong. And we all like to learn new skills; to expand our interests. Challenging mental activities stimulate, sharpen, and strengthen the mind.

Now here's an effective inner life exercise designed to help you grow and to develop greater **Spiritual Strength**: *No matter what happens, never blame anyone — or any thing — for the way you feel*. Rising above the blame game is the same as learning how to be in total command of yourself.

Now comes an interesting surprise. In this exercise about to be introduced, *it isn't what you do* that contributes to your Spiritual Strength: ***It's what you don't do*** that bestows the greatest gain. And, as you'll now learn, that's why it's your aim *not to blame* that finally bestows the new strength you seek.

This approach to enhancing inner strength through quiet self-negation may seem confusing at first, so before we arrive at the hands-on part of this new exercise, let's clear up any lingering questions you may have on the subject.

Q: What is Spiritual Strength?

A: Spiritual Strength is many things that really arise out of One. For the time being here are three correct answers, the last of which best serves our study together:

1. Spiritual Strength is the power to live spontaneously free while remaining alert and fully responsible to the need of the present moment.

2. Spiritual Strength is the courage to live exactly as you choose without the fear of being left out — or — of being left alone.

3. Spiritual Strength is the Higher Understanding that gives you the power *to **not*** act from spiritual weakness.

Q: What is spiritual weakness?

A: Any unconscious aspect of your nature which either causes you — or others — to suffer; or anything that interferes with your development of Spiritual Strength.

Q: What's the connection between blaming others for the way I feel and spiritual weakness?

A: Irritated inner states never seek solutions, only *reasons for why* they have a right to exist! By constantly feeding you "good reasons" as to why you feel badly, the weakness that blames others blinds you to your real inner condition: Which is going nowhere except 'round and down.

Q: What should I do?

A: The next time you feel yourself starting to become frustrated, angry or scared, do your best to confirm this next vital insight: ***Negative emotions can't exist without having something to blame for their punishing presence.***

The clearer for yourself you can make this spiritual fact — about the dualistic nature of spiritual weakness — the better prepared you'll be to take your next step toward higher Spiritual Strength. Your discovery leads you to this totally new action: *Whatever it takes*, do not express that surfacing irritation by naming, or blaming, anything *outside of you* as being its cause.

Even if you have to remove yourself physically from the developing situation, then just do it. Find some way to temporarily isolate yourself — *along with* your smoldering emotional state. Please note: "isolate yourself *along with* your agitation".

If it helps to make what appears to be a bitter pill taste better, think of these inner-trials as The Pause That Spiritually Strengthens; for a New Strength is exactly what you'll win for yourself each time you elect to work with this exercise. The powerful principles behind your coming success are further illuminated in the following.

Voluntarily isolating yourself along with your irritated thoughts and feelings doesn't mean to cut them off; nor does it mean that you should pretend that you're not on fire. Suppression of these weak inner states is just the opposite of angrily expressing them, and every bit as harmful. Don't express — or suppress — any negative state. Besides, either one of these opposite approaches always produces the same results: Nothing changes except for *what's* being blamed. Choosing to not blame lifts you above both of these losing choices.

Your conscious *non-action* turns you into the objective witness of what are your own super-heated emotions. And from the safety of this Higher awareness you see about yourself what you could not see before because of all the inner fire and smoke. Your discoveries empower you to cancel the real cause of your inner combustabilty. Not only is your self command restored, but it's heightened. For each discovery of an unseen weakness heralds the coming of a greater Spiritual Strength. Practice The Pause That Spiritually Strengthens. Refuse to blame.

"The strength of a man sinks in the hour of trial: But there doth live a power that to the battle girdeth the weak."

— *Joanna Baillie*

Special Summary

Choose to change right now, and you won't have to worry about how to be different next time.

Exercise # 8
ERASE THOSE FEARFUL FEELINGS

Special Insight

There is no such thing as a shaky situation, so any time you start to tremble, don't look *around you* for the fault: *Look inward.* It's the inner-ground you're standing on that isn't solid.

Exercise and Instruction

That seemingly scary condition, whatever it may be, is not the problem. It's your reaction that has you shaking. And that's why, if you'll become **conscious** of any fearful condition *instead of becoming afraid of it,* you'll change forever your relationship with fear. It's true.

Being conscious of your fear empowers you to interact with it in an entirely new way, because this new inner relationship gives you the power to **be awake** to its scary influences, instead of being their unconscious slave. And as each day you discover something new about the shaky nature of your own fearful reactions, they lose their power over you. Why? You see them for what they have always been: unintelligent mechanical forces.

To be consciously afraid means that *you know you are frightened,* but at the same time, to know that these very fears, as real as they may seem, *are not **you.***

Fear is really nothing other than a self-limiting reaction that we've always mistaken for a shield of self protection. It's time to let it go, which you can do anytime you want. Here's how: ***Just dare to proceed, even while being afraid.***

Employing this simple but higher instruction, *to proceed even while being afraid,* will not only show you the strange faces of all those habitual reactions that have had you on the run, but it will also empower you *to start seeing **through** them.* And, as you'll gratefully discover, each of your new insights into their actual nature removes some of their power over you. Better yet, their loss is your gain! Here now is the exercise that will help you face those fearful feelings and erase them from your life once and for all.

Do you know someone whom you would rather run from than run into? Most of us do! Nevertheless, starting right ***Now,*** resolve never again to avoid any person who scares you. In fact, whether at home or work, go ahead and walk right up to that critical man or aggressive woman and say exactly what *you* want, instead of letting the fear tell you to do what *it* wants. Have no ideas at all about the way things should or shouldn't go. Of course, this exercise is not an excuse to be cruel, or rude.

Remember, your aim in working with this exercise in self liberation is not to win an ego victory, but rather, to watch and learn something new *about yourself.* Drop any other misplaced self conscious concerns. Let that person see you shake, if that's what starts to happen. What do you care? It's only temporary. Besides, that unpleasant person before you can't know it, but you're shaking yourself awake!

Stand your inner ground even if it feels as though you might fall through the floor. Allow your reactions to roll by you — instead of letting them carry you away as they've always done in the past.

If you'll fight for yourself in this new way, it won't be the floor beneath you that you feel open. **It will be your inner eyes!** And what they see is that this flood — of what were once unconscious reactions — has its own life story; a shaky story that up until now you'd taken as your own. But it's not. You see these fears do not belong *to you*, and that ***they never have***. Everything about your life changes in this one moment. Here's what has been revealed to you.

You have never been afraid of another person. The only thing you've ever been frightened by is *your own **thoughts** about* that person. Yes, you did feel fear, but it wasn't yours. And it wasn't towards someone stronger than you. The fear you always felt was in what you *thought* he or she was thinking about you. Amazing isn't it? You have been afraid of your own thoughts.*

Facing your fearful feelings brings them to an end because, if you'll proceed while being afraid, you will see all that's been scaring you . . . *is you.*

* The Secret Of Letting Go, Guy Finley. Llewellyn, 1991

"There is great beauty in going through life

without anxiety or fear. Half our fears are

baseless, and the other half discreditable."

— Christian Bovee

Special Summary

You only have to enter the fear of the unknown once, while you must live the fear of pretending that you know with each pretence.

Exercise # 9
RELEASE AND RELAX YOURSELF

Special Insight

Natural and unrestricted energy is to your health, happiness, and spiritual development, what a snow-fed river is to a high mountain lake whose waters must be renewed each day.

Exercise and Instruction

Most people spend much of their lives in a constant struggle to hold themselves together. Even a brief glance shows us that a life spent in this futile fashion is most likely an unproductive one, because those energies that are meant to be poured into creative expression and continued self development, are used instead to just keep common things in place. So this special exercise, one of the author's favorites, *is all about letting yourself fall apart.*

Please! Don't be put off by the mere mention of this unusual approach to physical and spiritual re-vitalization. The energies that have been wasted in undetected physical tension, once released, will be re-directed to supply you with an abundant source of inner peace, higher intuition, and an unshakable sense of well-being. Would you like to know if there's really a secret way to let yourself go that will, at the same time, get you going — and doing — and feeling better than you have in a long time? Read on!

Each day we are allotted a certain amount of life-energy. In the East this inner force is called Chi; In India, Prana. The name of these energies varies by culture, but not the fact of its existence. If you doubt this daily distribution of life-force, ask yourself the following three questions, and then seriously ponder their answers.

1. Where does the energy come from that's allowing you to hold this book — or to have the thoughts and feelings you're experiencing right now?

2. Are you the source of the life-force that beats your heart, and that empowers you to take that breath you just took?

3. Are you the creator of your own animating energy, or are you *its* creation?

These answers should be clear.

The energy used to sustain our lives is given to us daily. But *how* those energies are used *is given to us* to decide. So this exercise is about making the conscious decision to **Relax And Release Yourself.**

With conscious effort you can learn to release those vital energies that are being wasted in undetected physical tension. What will liberating these natural forces do for you? Everything!

Imagine what happens to a flourishing orchard when the stream which naturally irrigates it is accidently blocked or diverted by a large, fallen boulder. The orchard is able to continue living, but not nearly to its potential. Growth is stunted; life held back.

Now imagine that obstructing rock being removed. The waters return, and with them the orchard's original vitality. New, vigorous growth is assured.

Common physical tension is a boulder that blocks — and wastes — our overall energies. Poor health, irritated nerves, and vague anxieties, are just a few of the ways blocked energies negatively impact our everyday lives. Here's a soothing and sound way to remove these invisible inner rocks and to realize refreshing new vitality.

At least three times a day, decide to relax and release yourself. Use the technique that follows, but don't get all tensed up trying to comply with a set of instructions. Remember: Freedom is natural. So, while on the road to self release, allow your natural interest, and the inner discoveries it reveals, to be your final guide.

When you first begin to practice this exercise, it may be to your advantage to find a comfortable place where you can be alone. But, before too long, you'll learn to apply this energy-releasing and life-renewing inner technique anywhere, any time, and under any circumstances.

Eventually, after you get the feel for it, you'll be able to do this exercise with your eyes open. But, for now, close your eyes and bring your attention to the top of your head. As you become aware of your scalp area, and those muscles that span across your forehead and temples, allow them to relax. Give these muscles a quiet mental command to let go, and then let them do as you've asked. If necessary (and most likely it will be) repeat this silent release instruction and letting-go action several times until you feel a definite response. *Don't get frustrated* if at first you don't succeed. Your muscles have probably been tense for so long they may not know how to relax, let alone remain at ease in that state. Nevertheless, stick with it.

In a few moments, or however long it may take, when your muscles yield to your decision to relax, you'll feel a pleasant sensation ease down from the crown of your head and continue to move downward along its sides. Give your complete attention to the inviting movement of this spreading relaxation and let yourself go with its gentle flow.

Now, *while remaining aware* of the forces you've set in motion, take the next step. Place your attention on the muscles all around — and particularly just beneath — your eyes. There's a tremendous amount of tension stored in this facial muscle group. In fact, these muscles right around the eyes may be so rigid that, at first mental survey, this whole area may feel as though its locked up, and unable to be released. Be patient with yourself, but do persist. This stubborn tension will yield.

As these energies are released you may feel some trembling or quivering in those areas, but have no concern. In time, as you continue to refine this exercise, so that these muscles remain relaxed all day long, you'll actually feel your entire facial structure start to change. There's a good chance your eyesight could improve. Who knows? You might even get better looking!

Continue to relax and release yourself by applying the same procedures just described to the area around your mouth. Then, as you stay in conscious touch with yourself to see that all previously released muscle groups are remaining at ease, go ahead and relax the neck, shoulders, chest, arms and hands, using the same basic technique of consciously deciding to relax that part of yourself.

If you want to, and time permits, relax and release yourself in this way all the way down to your toes. And if you have trouble falling off to sleep at night, this complete body release is especially helpful for inducing a deep relaxed state. You'll awaken more refreshed too.

It's always the right time to be relaxed. So create your own abbreviated form of these self release techniques, and learn to release and relax yourself while you're on the phone, watching TV, even when you're out dining with friends.

"If the mind, that rules the body, ever so far forgets itself as to trample on its slave, the slave is never generous enough to forgive the injury, but will rise and smite the oppressor."

— Henry Wadsworth Longfellow

Special Summary

Everyday: Casual, but industrious. Every moment: Relaxed, but alert.

Exercise # 10
STOP THIS SECRET SELF SABOTAGE

Special Insight

There is no pleasing the fear that you may displease others.

Exercise and Instruction

It's a little known, yet much denied, fact that people treat you the way you secretly asked to be treated. Your unspoken request, that determines how others behave towards you, is extended to — and received by — everyone you meet. This petition is broadcast, second by second, in the form of silent messages emanating from your own invisible inner life.

What is your invisible inner life? The way you *actually feel* — as opposed to the way you're trying to appear — when meeting any person or event. In other words, your invisible inner life is your *real* inner condition. It's this state of internal affairs that communicates with others long before any words are exchanged. These silent signals from your inner self are what a person receives first upon meeting you, and the reading of them determines, from that point forward, the basis of your relationship. This unseen dialogue that goes on behind the scenes whenever two or more people meet is commonly understood as 'sizing one another up'. But here's the point of this introduction.

We're often led to act against ourselves by an undetected weakness that goes before us — trying to pass itself off to others — as a strength. This is secret self sabotage. It sinks us in our personal and business relationships as surely as a torpedo wrecks the ship it strikes. Learning how to stop this self sinking is the focus of this exercise. So, let's begin by gathering the higher insights we'll need to succeed.

Any person you feel the need to control or dominate — so that he or she will treat you as you "think" you should be treated — will always be in charge of you . . . and treat *you* accordingly. Why? Because anyone from whom you want something, psychologically speaking, is always in secret command of you. The dynamics of this spiritual law are revealed in the following paragraph.

It would never dawn on any person to want to be more powerful, or superior to someone else, unless there was some psychic character within him or her that secretly felt itself to be weaker, or lessor, than that other individual. From where else would such a petty concern originate if not out of an unseen, unsettling feeling of inferiority? Genuine inner strength neither competes, nor compares itself to others, any more than an eagle wants to fly like a crow or waddle like a duck. Neither real strength, nor regal eagle, have any need to prove anything.

What this important lesson teaches us is that any

action we take *to appear* strong before another person is actually read by that person as a weakness. If you doubt this finding, review the past interactions and results of your own relationships. The general rule of thumb is that the more you demand, or crave, the respect of others, the less likely you are to receive it. If you've ever tried to raise children you know this is true.

So, you see, it makes no sense to try and change the way others treat you by learning calculated behaviors, or attitude techniques, in order to *appear* in charge. The only thing these clever cover-ups really produce is yet another source of secret inner conflict; which, in turn, only fuels further self sabotage. Besides, what you're really looking for in your relationships isn't command over others — **but over yourself.** So what's the answer?

Stop trying to be strong, and instead, start catching yourself about to act from weakness.

Don't be too surprised by this unusual instruction. A brief examination reveals its wisdom. Following are ten examples of where you may be secretly sabotaging yourself while wrongly assuming you're strengthening your position with others.

1. Fawning before someone to win his favor.

2. Expressing contrived concern for her well-being.

3. Making small talk to smooth out the rough edges.

4. Hanging onto his every word.

5. Looking for her approval.

6. Asking if he's angry with you.

7. Fishing for a kind word.

8. Trying to impress another.

9. Gossiping.

10. Explaining yourself to others.

Let's look at this last act of secret self sabotage on our list, and use it to see how we can transform what has always been the seed of some self sinking act into a conscious source of self command.

The next time you feel as though you need to explain yourself to someone, other than to your employer as it may concern his or her business affairs, give yourself this one, quick and simple internal test. It will help you check for, and then cancel, any undetected weakness that's about to make you sabotage yourself. Here's what to do: **Run a pressure check**. Here's how.

Inwardly scan yourself to see if that question you're about to answer — or that answer you're about to give, without having been asked for it — *is something **you really want to do**. Or, are you about to explain yourself because you're afraid of some, as yet undisclosed, consequence *if you don't*?

This self-administered test for inner pressure is how you tell if your forthcoming explanation is truly voluntary, or if you're on the verge of being shanghaied again into an unconscious act of self sabotage. Your awareness of any pressure building within you is the proof that it's some form of *fear* — and *not you* — that wants to do the explaining; or the fawning; or the impressing; or the blabbing; or whatever the self sabotaging act it may be that that inner pressure is pushing you to commit.

Each time you feel this pressurized urge to give yourself away, silently, but solidly, refuse to release this pressure by giving into its demands. It may just help you to succeed sooner if you know that *fear has no voice unless it tricks you into giving it one.* So stay silent. Your conscious silence stops self sabotage.

"In all our weaknesses we have one element of strength if we recognize it. Here, as in other things, knowledge of danger is often the best means of safety."

— *E.P. Roe*

Special Summary

In any and every given moment of your life, you are either in command of yourself . . . or you are being commanded.

Exercise # 11
GO QUIET

Special Insight

The frantic search for any answer only delivers answers on the same frantic level.

Exercise and Instruction

One of the most powerful forces in the universe available to human beings is also one of the least understood and appreciated. The subject of this exercise is *Silence*.

The wise words of Richard Cecil, an 18th century English author and theologian, set the stage for our study and invite us to begin.

"The grandest operations, both in nature and Grace, are the most silent and imperceptible. The shallow brook babbles in its passage and is heard by everyone; but the coming of the seasons is silent and unseen. The storm rages and alarms, but its fury is soon exhausted, and its effects are but partial and soon remedied; but the dew, though gentle and unheard, is immense in quantity, and is the very life of large portions of the earth. And these are pictures of the operations of Grace in the church and in the soul."

But don't be mislead. Reach no conclusions about the true nature of what is quiet. The secret strength of silence can be as practical in your everyday life as is its real character to be life changing. You can actually have — and benefit directly from — a quiet mind.

To help bring this important and higher self-possibility down to earth, I've prepared a list of 25 powers that can be directly attributed to a mind that has found real silence. Be amazed! And then take action. The exercise that follows this list places you on the inner road that leads to the source of these true strengths.

A Quiet Mind:

1. Is spontaneously creative in any situation

2. Can neither betray itself, nor anyone else

3. Rests naturally when it isn't naturally active

4. Knows without thinking

5. Seeks nothing outside of itself for strength

6. Detects and easily rejects psychic intruders

7. Never compromises itself

8. Can not be flattered or tempted

9. Doesn't waste valuable energy

10. Fears nothing

11. Can't outsmart itself

12. Is never the victim of its own momentum

13. Refreshes itself

14. Is in relationship with a Higher Intelligence

15. Never struggles with painful thoughts

16. Is instantly intuitive

17. Gives its undivided attention to its tasks

18. Receives perfect direction from within

19. Deeply enjoys the delight of its own quietness

20. Lives above expectations and disappointments

21. Can't be captured by regrets

22. Commands every event it meets

23. Lives in a state of Grace

24. Never feels lonely

25. Knows, and helps to create, its own destiny

When you want to directly enjoy the sunshine you must go outdoors. You understand you have to take yourself physically to a place where the warming rays of the sun can fall upon you without interference.

Likewise, when you want to know the powers that circulate through a quiet mind, you must take yourself to that place where this Silent Strength can make itself known to you. *To go quiet, you must go within.*

In those days now past, when Christ told his disciples to seek the Kingdom of Heaven within, his words of Wisdom were not the religion they've become today. They were alive with secret, but ever-so-practical, instructions how a person could discover, and realize, a secret part of him- or herself that was not a part of what was then — and of what still remains — a conflict-torn and weary world. This Master Instruction still holds true. If we want to know that stillness; that silent strength; a peace that passeth all understanding, we must go within. We must go quiet. Now, here's how.

The best time to practice going quiet is when the world around you is already in a natural state of silence. So, early morning, upon arising, and just before you go to sleep, are the most likely times to yield the best results. But, as you'll no doubt come to discover for yourself, **any time is the right time** to go quiet.

Find a place to sit where your back can be more or less supported and held straight. Let your hands rest, open or closed, in any position that won't cause tension to themselves, your arms or shoulders, as you remain seated for the duration of your practice. Twenty to thirty minutes, twice a day, is a suggested minimum time to sit quietly. But do the best you can. There are no laws that govern inner silence. Besides, the day may come when you'd like to sit for longer durations, so you be the judge. Let the length of this time for inner quiet be whatever it wants to be.

Allow your legs to assume whatever position is most naturally relaxed for them. It's better if you don't cross your legs one over the other, as this posture interferes with your circulation, and the ensuing discomfort will become a distraction.

Once your body is situated and in relative ease, close your eyes and let your awareness sweep over the whole of your body. Adjust your limbs again, if necessary, so that no individual part of your physical self is calling out for your attention.

Now, with your eyes still gently closed, let your shoulders take the full weight of your head. You should actually be able to feel the physical transfer of this weight take place.

Then, give the weight of your shoulders and your arms to the armrests of your chair, or to whatever part of your body is beneath them. If you're doing this properly, you'll be surprised how much of your own bodily weight you were unnecessarily supporting without knowing it! Finally, give all of this collective weight — head, shoulders, arms, upper body, buttocks and legs — to the chair or sofa you're sitting upon. Consciously transfer the weight. Let it go. Then let yourself sink into the feeling that comes with releasing all this unconscious physical stress and tension.

The next step is to continue expanding this relaxed and increased awareness of your body to include within it the awareness of your thoughts and feelings. In other words, bring into your enhanced physical awareness the further awareness of what your mind and emotions are doing in the moment. You watch *yourself.*

This form of self observation is as interesting as it is challenging. To ensure your success in this phase of going within and going quiet, consider yourself as being a naturalist of the mind.

A good wildlife naturalist casually observes the diverse ways of birds or bunnies without interfering. In order to study and learn, he or she just watches. And that's what you must learn to do as you journey within. You're to be an impartial witness to the life of your own thoughts and feelings. Let them fly and hop around within you without the slightest concern for their direction or character. Neither resist, nor let yourself be drawn into any of their attention-stealing antics.

Again, all you want to do is watch. Detached self observation is your aim. So each time it comes to you to realize that you're no longer watching, but rather that you've been captured by a thought or feeling, and are being carried along by it, just quietly withdraw yourself from that temporary psychic wave. Come back to the awareness of yourself in the Present Moment. This part of your practice is the heart and soul of going — and knowing — quiet. You must experience it for yourself. So, as you sit: Let go; give up; go within, and watch. And over and over again, bring your awareness of yourself back into the awareness of the Present Moment.

One special way to help "ground" yourself in the **Now** is to use your awareness of each out-breath as a reminder to give all of your weight back to the chair. So, each time you breathe out, let yourself go, completely. Stay watchful and consciously drop the heaviness of your body, mind and emotions. *Let something else* be responsible for their weight. This is the greatest feeling in the world, and it prepares you for the eventual Higher stages of this exercise.

And pay no attention to what your own thoughts and feelings are trying to tell you the whole time you're sitting. Which is namely this: "You should give up this worthless, unproductive practice!" Learn to watch, and drop, these dark inner voices. They don't want you to succeed. You see, they can't dwell in that silent world you wish to enter, and that wishes to enter you.

So persist! You **will** prevail. For even as you struggle to stay aware of yourself in the Present Moment, that moment itself, changes. And as it does, so do you.

Slowly, subtly at first, but eventually even beyond those protestations raised by your own mind, the distinction between your sense of self and your awareness of the Present Moment melts away. And as it does, a new, deeper sense of silence floods into you; filling your awareness with itself and, at the same time, with yet another Awareness that the source of this supreme stillness *is arising out of your own **Being***. It washes everything out of its way. And so arrives a quiet mind.

"The sovereignty of nature has been allotted to the silent forces. The moon makes not the faintest echo of a noise, yet it draws millions of tons of tidal waters to and fro at its biding. We do not hear the sun rise, nor the planets set. So, too, the dawning of the greatest moment in a man's life comes quietly, with none to herald it to the world. In that Stillness alone is born the knowledge of the Overself. The gliding of the mind's boat into the lagoon of the spirit is the gentlest thing I know; it is more hushed than the fall of eventide."

— *Dr. Paul Brunton*

Special Summary

Just as you can see farther on a clear day, new understanding flowers in a quiet mind.

Note: For extra benefit, employ exercise # 9, *Release And Relax Yourself,* during this exercise.

Set Your Sights On Self Liberation

*T*hese eleven inner life exercises share one life-changing objective in common. They are all about awakening you to new and Higher levels of yourself through increased *self awareness*. But, as you proceed with your studies and practices, please, always keep this one, very important, fact before your enquiring mind: There is no scale, no measuring stick for this new inner awareness, any more than you can measure the Cosmos.

What this means is that in our inner work to awaken and realize ourselves, we must begin where we begin, and put away any other concerns about where that beginning is. It's enough just to make a start, wherever that may be. What difference does it make at what point you enter into a great river? Sooner or later, *all* of its waters reach and pour into the sea.

Never let discouragement have the final word, and one day there will be nothing left to discuss. Besides, you can have just as many new beginnings as you're willing to leave behind all of your ideas about yourself. Nothing is this world, or in any other, can stop you from discovering your

Original, Free Being. This has always been your destiny, as Walt Whitman confirms:

"The central urge in every atom, to return to its divine source and origin."

As a final review and summary of the important lessons in this book, following are 10 secret ways higher self studies help you succeed in life.

1. Higher self studies reveal that your nature is your fortune, so better luck begins with a *change of self.*

2. Higher self studies hold many benefits for the sincere student, like the deep-sea diver who discovers a treasure chest lying buried beneath a bed of pearls.

3. Higher self studies introduce your mind to a Higher Body of Wisdom whose elevated Nature lifts you, as wind does the wings of an eagle.

4. Higher self studies prove that permitting your life direction to be determined by the way the world turns is like using the pointer of a wind-lashed weather vane for your compass and guide.

5. Higher self studies prove that changing the way you see life changes the life you see.

6. Higher self studies pave the happy and relief-filled way to a new life that isn't governed by ceaseless compromise and painful self interest.

7. Higher self studies reveal secret sources of conflict, as in discovering that the chief thief responsible for stealing *your peace of mind is your own certainty that **you already know** the real nature of security.*

8. Higher self studies provide superior self safety by helping you develop a new awareness that can see through highly reflective surfaces, as in well-polished personalities that conceal hidden motives.

9. Higher self studies teach you the Wisdom of letting go, which has nothing to do with giving up on your life — or into your desires.

10. Higher self studies make it clear that looking for a sense of self permanence in the way others think about you is like trying to make a plaster cast of the wind.

A Special Note To The Reader

You're invited to write to the author with comments or questions about *The Key Of Kings*.

Guy Finley lives and teaches in Southern Oregon. For free information on books, tapes, and friendly on-going classes, write to: The Life Of Learning Foundation, PO Box 170 KK, Merlin, Oregon 97532

Help spread the Light. Send us the names of anyone you know who might be interested in these Higher Ideas, and we'll send him or her the above information.

To receive **30 Keys To Change Your Destiny,** a powerful 28-page pocket-book version of the inner life exercises in *The Key Of Kings*, plus nineteen more fascinating and self empowering discoveries, Send a # 10 SASE, along with $2, to:

Life Of Learning, PO Box 170 KB, Merlin, Oregon, 97532. Outside the U.S. send $3. U.S. funds only.

If you enjoyed reading the new and self liberating material in *The Key Of Kings*, you won't want to miss reading Guy Finley's life-changing book, **Freedom From The Ties That Bind** (a Llewellyn Worldwide Publication, February, 1994.)